System Design

Interview

System Design Interview

A Strategic Guide for a Successful Interview

Stanley Bellbrook

Introduction

Why should you read this book? You likely know everything there is to know about system design – anyone who has ever taken a programming class knows how easy it is. So, why waste your time to make sure that you've got it all covered? Why not jump straight into the system design interview (SDI) questions and save yourself some trouble? The answer is obvious; system design is *anything* but simple.

If you think about it, even Microsoft has had projects that were overdue or complete failures (think Windows 95 or Windows 1.0), so why are you so convinced that you will succeed on your very first try?

Don't get me wrong – this book is not a magic bullet that will save you from failing at designing systems. It is, however, closer to 'magic' than any other designing method you might try. Only thorough knowledge and practical techniques will increase your chance of developing a killer system design – both of which are covered in this book. That is why you should read this book – to nail your system design interview.

Being interviewed for any job is a challenging process, but shooting for a top-tier IT firm, now that's downright intimidating. But not if you know exactly what to expect. Take a dive into this book to explore the depths of system design. Learn effective design techniques; how to approach your SDI the right way; and be prepared for any question the interviewer might ask.

System design may be a standard requirement for an IT interview, but trust me, if you can provide a top-notch system design, you will be given anything but a standard work position.

So, what are you waiting for? Every chapter will bring you one step closer to your dream job. Start reading and make your dreams happen!

Chapter 1:

The System Development Life Cycle

Just like you cannot jump straight into decorating the interior of your house before putting a roof over the building, you cannot design a system if you fail to go through some other steps first. While you may think building a house and designing a system cannot possibly be the same, these two have more in common than you may think.

Think about the way a house is built for a second. Building a house, just like the system, starts with a simple idea. Then, the owner presents that idea to a developer, who then transforms the vision into a drawing. The simple drawing is then – most likely – refined through a couple of sketches, until the owner decides that the drawing entails everything that they want in their house. Next, the developer produces detailed blueprints that give the simple drawing much more specific information (electrical outlets, final room layout, plumbing, etc.). Finally, the process of building the house can start.

Just like building a house, the System Development Life Cycle (SDLC) also has a set of fundamental phases. Of course, not all projects are built the same way. Different approaches may be taken and different parts can be emphasized, however, one thing remains consistent – all projects contain elements of the four SDLC phases.

Planning

The initial phase of developing a system is to figure out whether the system is worth building in the first place and to determine further steps that the team should take to start the building process. This phase is called *planning*, and it has two steps:

1. *Initiation* – During this step, the team identifies if the system can bring any value to the organization in order to see whether it is worth developing. At this step, the team analyzes the feasibility:

   - The technical feasibility – Can the team build it?
   - The economic feasibility – Will the system bring business value?
   - The organizational feasibility – If the team builds it, will the system be used?

2. *Project Management* – When the *approval committee* gives the green light and decides that the system is indeed worth building, then the idea takes on more meaning and enters project management. The project manager, then, creates the work plan for the system; gives assignments to the staff; and directs the process of system development towards the other phases of SDLC.

Analysis

The *analysis* phase is when questions are finally answered such as: *What will it do? Who are the*

users? When and where will the system be implemented?
The analysis phase is made of three steps:

1. *Analysis Strategy* – During this stage, the team analyzes the current system and inspects not only its issues, but also its benefits to gain a clear picture of how the new system should be designed to increase value.

2. *Gathering Requirements* – The requirements for the system design are usually gathered through questionnaires and interviews, and allow the analysts to develop a concept for their system. Once that is completed, the system concept is used to develop analysis models to show how the business will most likely operate once the system is developed.

3. *System Proposal* - This proposal is basically a document that contains the concept, the models, and the analyses for the new system. The system proposal is a formal way of presenting the information that the team has gathered to those that will approve or deny the development (ie: project sponsors).

Design

Although we will talk about this phase in greater detail throughout this book, it would be a remiss to not explain it here briefly. The *design* phase will determine exactly how the system will operate – not only in terms of software, but also hardware and network infrastructure as well. User interfaces will be developed and requirements for files and databases will be established.

The design phase has four steps:

1. *Design Strategy* – During this step, it is clarified who will program the system. Will the company use its own programmers? Will they buy a packaged software? Or will they hire another firm to do the programming on their behalf?

2. *Architecture Design* – This step describes the exact software, hardware and network infrastructure that should be used. The way in which the team will move through the system and which reports the system will use is described in the *interface design*.

3. *Database and File Specifications* – This step determines the data that the system will use and the place where that data will be stored.

4. *Program Design* – During the program design phase, it is determined which programs should be written and what these programs will do.

Implementation

Implementation is the final phase of the SDLC and it represents the phase in which the system gets built. This phase of the SDLC gets the most attention as it is the most important, the longest, and, needless to say, the most expensive phase.

The implementation phase has three steps:

1. *Construction* – The team programs the system during this step. While it may seem like the most important part, it is the testing, not the coding, that gets the most attention. The company must make sure that the system works smoothly, since bugs often carry immense costs.

2. *Installation* – As the name suggests, installation means turning on the new system. This can be done by replacing the old system completely; by allowing users to operate both systems in parallel to ensure that there are no bugs; or by installing the system in only one area and then gradually rolling it out to other areas. As important as this seems, it is equally important to develop a training plan so the users can be taught how to use the new system.

3. *Support Plan* – These are the reviews and feedback that the system will receive. This plan is established by the analysts and can be either a formal or informal way of soliciting user reviews. This is when any changes to the system – whether minor or major – are identified.

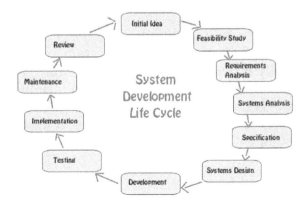

First, Analyze!

If you are confused why we are explaining the analysis phase and not jumping straight into designing the system, it is because the line that separates these two phases can be very thin. If you think about it, analysis can be viewed as an initial step of the design rather than a phase on its own. As we said earlier, during the analysis, we take care of the strategic decisions. No wonder some organizations refer to this phase as 'Analysis and Initial Design'.

Being a precursory step of design, the analysis phase is critical for the whole system since it is concerned with the future of the design. After all, if the analysis is not executed correctly, the SDLC will not proceed to the design phase.

Imagine the work load of the analyst. Besides needing strong interpersonal and analytical skills in order to build a proper system, the analysts also have to choose the *method of system development*.

The traditional approach to system development was the so-called structured design. This design became dominant in the 1980s and was a much more practical and beneficial approach than the previous ad hoc design. The structured design included a step-by-step approach to the whole cycle of system development and logically moved from one phase to the next. This approach meant consulting users only when absolutely necessary and when their feedback was required. As you can probably imagine, a lot of things were lacking with this method.

As things progressed, so did this old-fashioned, one-way approach. Today, the goal of the IT department remains to deliver the best possible system in the shortest amount of time and for the lowest possible cost. Today, however, this is done in collaboration with the users. Today, the IT department is much more user-approached, meaning that IT companies look at users as partners. After all, the greater the communication, the better the development and the more positive the results.

The most popular approaches to system development today are:

Joint Application Development (JAD)

This approach is a great fact-finding technique that engages users in the development process and encourages their active participation. This will give the users a sense of ownership which will increase their support for the new system.

The most successful method for user involvement is a team approach of JAD. The JAD team - users, IT professionals, and managers – usually meets weekly to discuss the progress of the project.

Rapid Application Development (RAD)

As you can imagine, this method of system development involves speeding things up and building a system in a shorter timeframe. RAD also uses a group approach, but unlike JAD, RAD is a complete methodology that doesn't have the requirement model, and instead, uses the new information system as the final goal.

This method consists of having the users examine the prototype in a relatively short amount of time to determine which changes they want made.

The Agile Method

The agile method emphasizes constant feedback. It consists of developing the system incrementally, building a series of prototypes, and constantly making the required changes. Here, the developers revise, extend, and merge the previous system versions into a final and ready product.

Today, there is a large community of agile software and services, so chances are, the company that you will be interviewed for is also agile oriented.

Now that you know why the analysis phase is so important for your system design, let's dive into more details on how we can gather the necessary equipment – the requirements

The Requirements

Determining the requirements is perhaps the most important part of the whole SDLC. It is the starting point from where all the important elements of the system emerge. At this stage, the system has not yet evolved and so it is fairly easy to change course and decide to move in a different direction if some features are not working to our satisfaction. As the system moves through the design and then implementation, making changes is a lot more difficult and costly. To put it simply, making changes during the subsequent phase means that we've failed to determine the right requirements and now have to go back and rework the system.

Of course, taking the Agile approach may save you from redoing things since this methodology consists of identifying and implementing small batches of requirements in incremental stages, however, the requirements determination is still the most important step of all. Mastering this area can have a significant impact on the success of your system design interview.

So, what kind of requirements are we talking about? A requirement is a statement of the things that the system should have or do. They can either be *functional* or *non-functional* in nature. People often use these terms interchangeably, so let me explain them briefly and in plain English.

A *functional requirement* is something that the system should do. Typically, these requirements specify a function or a behavior. Think of a coat. Its functional requirements are to cover your upper body and keep you warm.

A n*onfunctional requirement* explains how the system works and specify how it should behave. Take the coat as an example. The nonfunctional requirement of a raincoat, for instance, would be that 'it must not absorb water'.

In terms of software, things get a little bit more complex than a simple raincoat, however, once you learn how to determine the real requirements, the result will be much more successful.

During the analysis phase, the requirements are determined from a business perspective, meaning that they should be focused on what the system should *do* to satisfy user needs. These user and functional requirements may be determined during the analysis phase but they flow into the Design phase where they evolve and take on more technical meaning, describing how the system will be used.

Use Case

You cannot possibly determine the correct system requirements if you fail to understand the user's requirements first. So, the key to success → satisfy the user.

Use cases are used to express the requirements of the users and are established during the analysis phase through interviews, questionnaires, and workshops.

In the past, determining the user's requirements meant simply asking the users what they wanted from the system. But, as straightforward and simple as this may seem, there were many issues with this strategy. For starters, most of the time, the users were not fully aware of system capabilities and constraints. Another issue was that some users were not able to truly understand the limitations of IT. Others found it hard to envision the redesigning process.

Thus, the use case has evolved into a powerful tool for determining requirements, regardless of the chosen development methodology.

Use case is a set of activities and processes that are used to achieve a desired result. It represents the way in which the system 'communicates' with its environment by demonstrating the activities that the users perform, as well as the responses of the system. They are usually considered to be a functional or an external view of a process, meaning that the users are more concerned with the processes than the mechanism under which they operate.

The use cases describe how a user can trigger a certain event to which the system will respond. For instance, think of a library system. The users borrow then return the books. The book can either be returned on time or it becomes overdue. When the book is in the library, the system will be 'at rest', waiting for someone to trigger the event and borrow the book.

In most situations, the event is rather quick. They are simple use cases because there is only one path. However, what happens if the book gets lost or damaged? That requires a slightly more complex system, because yet another event gets triggered. Now we have another possible path and the use case here requires several scenarios.

Writing a Use Case

Writing an effective use case and including all its possible steps may seem like a daunting task, but it doesn't have to be. The main things you need to focus on are the users, what they want, and what they might do.

#1: Define the Elements

Use cases are all about possible scenarios. They specify how a user uses your system and the things that happen when the system fails or succeeds. Every possible scenario is a different procedure. Here are the elements of a use case:

Users – Anyone who takes part in the activities and interacts with the system are called users. For instance, in a library system, the users are all the library members that borrow books.

Preconditions – These are all the elements that are in place before the use case starts. Think of Facebook, for instance. One of its preconditions is the fact that you don't have to retype your e-mail address every time you log in. You have logged in previously and now your computer has memorized your address – that is a precondition.

Basic Flow – Basic flow refers to both the procedure by which the users accomplish their goal and the related system reaction. For instance, you enter the correct password and Facebook allows access to your account.

Alternate Flow – This is an action that is less common, but still necessary. Think about inputting your e-mail address and password from another device. The system recognizes the new device and instead asks you a security question prior to granting access. That is an alternate flow.

Exception Flow – When the users fail to achieve their goal, the exception flow happens. Entering an incorrect password would be an example of this.

Post Conditions – All the elements that are present after the use case has been completed are called post conditions. Think about using Facebook after you log in.

#2: Define the User Implementation

Every possible thing that the user can do represents a separate use case. Depending on what the system is about, you can create many different use cases. For instance, if your system is about making online purchase orders, your use cases may be about:

- How the users log in to your system
- How the users enter their payment information
- How the users place their orders
- How to run sales reports, etc.

The point is to make sure that all functions of the business/technology under analysis get listed and a corresponding use case is written for each one of them.

#3: Define the Usual Course of Events

When writing a use case, you need to think about what the normal events are. That means that you need to outline everything that the user does and how the system responds to each of the user's actions. For instance, if you have a use case about logging into a system, the usual course of events would be the user entering their username or e-mail address and password, and the system responding to that information by denying or granting the user access.

Here, you also need to think about the alternate flows and exception flows and what happens if the user comes across an obstacle and cannot log in.

If, for example, the system doesn't recognize the user's computer, the user might be asked to verify their identity in some way. Another example would be if the user enters invalid information or have maybe forgotten their password. In that case, they might be prompted to enter their e-mail address, give the answer to their security question, and receive new password to log in.

#4: Repeat the Steps

You will need to think about all the separate functions and different users, repeat these steps, and write use cases for every scenario. You must first identify the user for each function, determine the usual course of events, and write the use cases accordingly. Keep in mind that the obstacles should also be considered and the contingencies must be explained well. The system's response to each step must also be well explained, since it represents the cornerstone of every use case.

Now that you know the steps to writing use cases, you just need to keep things in order and be effective. Here are the three keys to writing effective use cases:

#1: Capture What the Business Does

You need to be aware that the use case explains *the goal* of the business (or technology), not the way in which the business functions. That means that when writing a use case about logging into a system, for example, you need to keep your focus on what the user will do and how the system will respond. You are not concerned about the technical components or, let's say, the code in which the system is written.

Also, be careful with the details. For instance, about logging into a system, you shouldn't exclude the details about how the system will respond to the user entering their log in information. If you do that, you are simply writing a description of the process, not a use case.

Similarly, including too much detail is also not right. If you focus too much on system functionality, that is also not a use case; it will read like some sort of system design implementation. Getting the details right is critical.

#2: Keep it Textual

The use case should be simple and easy to understand. In other words, it should be easy to read and comprehend without needing a special level of training. It should be primarily textual; not packed with complex diagrams and charts. Some flow charts can be included if you feel like that will better clarify the information, however, keep any diagrams to a minimum.

#3: Learn the Most Important Details

A good use case should be able to let you know how the software or technology works. It should be able to educate readers on the proper vocabulary and terminology. By learning the most important details, this will ensure that you are using all the technical terms correctly in order to provide value to others.

User Story

User stories are part of the Agile methodology and they help transition from writing about the requirements, to talking about them. These stories are short, no longer than one or two sentences, and contain a series of conversation about the functionality that is expected.

User stories are simple and short feature descriptions that are told from the perspective of that person who expects to be provided with the new capability – which is usually the user or the customer.

They are the most powerful way to capture the functionality of a product. However, telling proper and effective stories can be tricky. Here are some considerations when writing user stories:

The User Always Comes First

There's a well-known expression *"The customer is always right"*. User stories are something like that. User stories represent the way in which the customer/user employs the product, and the user story is always told from the user's perspective. If you want your system to be successful, then it must be able to satisfy the users. Essentially, the user story is a description of what the customer wants from that product.

In order to write effective user stories, you must know who your customers are. If not, make sure that you do all the necessary research and interviews upfront to avoid creating user stories that are based on beliefs, and not on evidence.

Use Personas

Building user stories around personas is an amazing technique that allows you to better grasp the user's insight. But what are personas? Personas are fictional characters that should be based on the knowledge you have about the target group. This knowledge could be the user's name, other relevant characteristics, habits, attitudes, and most importantly – their goal. The goal is what that persona wants to achieve, and your job is to provide it.

The main thing that you should consider when creating user stories is what your product should do to address the user's problems and how to satisfy their goals.

Create Them Collaboratively

User stories are not a specification, but merely a collaboration tool. They should never be handed off to your development team. They are to be used in conversations between the product owner and their team. It is recommended to solicit team input when creating user stories.

They Should be Simple and Concise

When writing user stories, you should only focus on important details. Everything else should be left out. Strive to make them as clear and concise as possible, use an active voice, and keep things simple.

A proper user story could be written this way:

As a < the type of user >, I want to < the goal of the user >, so that < the reason/benefit>.

This is a great template to guide you. For instance, if you are developing a software that can help people backup their files. An effective user story can be something like this:

As a mom, I want to be able to backup my children's photos, so that I will not lose them.

As a user, I can select which files to backup manually, so that my backup isn't filled with files I do not need.

Breaking Down the Epics

You can write your user stories to cover multiple functionalities. We call these large user stories – epics. In the example above, the epic would be *As I user, I want to backup my data and protect it.* But because epics are large and may be too general, we can dive into the specifics and break them down, just like we did earlier.

So *"As I user, I want to backup my data and protect it"*, can become:

"As a user, I can select which files to backup manually, so that my backup isn't filled with things I do not need."

"As a user, I can specify the folders I want to backup based on data and file size, for more convenience."

Use Paper Cards

Did you know that in the early XP literature, they didn't use the term 'user stories' but instead used 'story cards'? That is because user stories were always captured on cards. And that is one very successful approach. Firstly, writing your user stories on cards is easy and cheap. Secondly, this is visually more appealing. Lastly, displaying user stories on cards will allow everyone in the team to participate and jot down ideas.

The main thing is to keep your stories visible and easily accessible, and not hidden on some drive. This will not only foster collaboration, but it will also increase productivity.

Constraints

There is a debate whether the constraints fall under the functional or non-functional requirements. However, the basket in which you place your constraints is not as important as knowing exactly why and when you need them. Know this – constraints are usually specified after the other functional requirements have been approved and they specify how the system should be built.

In system design, the term *constraints* can be defined as the practice that limits the actions of the user on the system. By limiting the actions that are performed by the users, the constraints reduce the chances for operating errors, and in turn, improve the usability of the system design.

The constraints can either be physical or psychological.

Physical Constraints

Physical constraints, as the name suggests, refers to using a physical object to constrain the user's actions. These physical objects can be:

Paths – They restrict the action of the users with a linear (or curvilinear) motion. This can be an extremely useful tool where there is a small control variable range. Just think of the volume bar on iTunes. It would be difficult to misuse that module, don't you agree?

Axes – Axes are there to direct the action of the user in a rotary motion. The most beneficial thing about this constraint is that it allows you to expand the control in length, and yet still allow it to exist in a very small space. Think of Illustrate CS6 and its rotate tool. It allows you to rotate the objects for 360 degrees thanks to the axis control that is there to guide your movement.

Barriers – The barriers redirect the actions of the users. They can slow and cease the non-conductive user actions and transform them into a much more successful experience. A good example of this is a dialog box that asks "Are you sure you want to take this action", which is popular for e-commerce platforms. Another example is a popup window that asks you to sign in to a website with your e-mail or Facebook account in order to continue reading and exploring.

Psychological Constraint

The psychological constraint limits the actions of the users by leveraging how the environment is perceived by people. There are three ways in which this constraint can be executed:

Symbols – Used for creating categories, making things clear, as well as warning people about particular actions, the symbols can communicate though sounds, text, and icons. For instance, think about the error sound your PC makes when there is an invalid entry. This sound is warning you to make a correction.

Conventions – This limits the actions with the help of the familiar exercises and customs. Think about a green and red button found next to each other. The implication of green (go) compared with red (stop) is clear.

Mappings – Mappings can limit the actions by creating an apparent relationship between two elements of a same design. For instance, think of a group of radio buttons that are placed next to a list of certain choices. The implied relationship is clear.

Perhaps to some, using constraints seems counter-intuitive, since it restricts the actions instead of enabling them, but implementing constraints can indeed aid in usability. Make sure to keep that in mind during your system design interview, as constraints may be one of the critical topics.

Chapter 2:

The Functional Side of System Design

Just like you cannot build a house before gathering the building material, you cannot build a system design without gathering all the important requirements. Now that we have covered that part, we can safely proceed to making the blueprint for our future system.

There is no better starting point than the most obvious – the functional specifications. A functional specification describes the behavior of the system that is externally visible.

If you try to explain a system in the simplest way possible, you can say that it has two main features:

1. Interface – through which the users can interact with the system via inputs and outputs.

2. State – the state is the system memory, which is basically the *data* that changes as a result of the system's interaction with the users

So yes, in case you were wondering, before we delve deeply into learning how to design large scale systems, we need to learn the functional part of the system design. In this case, that is the *User Interface Design* and *Database Design*.

User Interface (UI) Design

The user interface represents the way in which the user interacts with the system, as well as the nature of the inputs that the system accepts, and the outputs that it produces. The UI design is focused on anticipating the things that the user might do, as well as on making sure that the interface contains elements that are easy to access and use, in order to enable those actions.

The interface element includes, but is not limited to:

- <u>Navigational Components</u> such as menus, sliders, search fields, etc. This represents how the user gives the system instructions.

- <u>Input Controls</u> such as buttons, toggles, list boxes, text fields, dropdown lists, date fields, checkboxes, etc. This represents the way in which the system captures the information from the users.

- <u>Output or Informational Components</u> such as progress bars, message boxes, notifications, etc. This represents how the system gives information to the user.

When different elements are used to display the content, you might consider these as *trade-offs*. For instance, some elements may require you to guess the element so that you can save some space.

Even though there are many tips you can consider when designing a UI, the main thing – before all – is to know who are your users and what they want. Once that is established, you can take advantage of these tips:

Keep it Simple. Did you know that the best interfaces are those that the user cannot even see? They are not packed with unnecessary elements or language and are clear and simple. Keep that in mind.

Be Consistent. You should always play it safe and use the most common (previously mentioned) UI elements, but perhaps even more important, you should learn how to be consistent. For instance, if you use an icon for one purpose, do not use the same icon for another purpose. Make sure that the user is comfortable, and remember, their goal is to get things done quickly and effectively.

Prevent Errors. Strive to design the systems in a way that will keep the errors to a minimum. No one likes the 'problem detected' message, so be sure to eliminate (or flag!) any actions that might result in an error.

Aesthetics and Minimalism. Keep things clean, neat, and aesthetically appealing. Clutter should be avoided and the display should not be packed with unnecessary components.

Better User Control. Make sure to offer users digital shortcuts and include keys for 'undo' and 'redo' functions.

Be Strategic. Take advantage of the textures and colors to draw the user's attention where you want it most.

Be Specific About the Defaults. Creating default settings takes a huge weight from the user's shoulders. Make sure to plan and think this through well, as most users will probably depend on these settings (at least for some time).

There are five steps in the process of designing a User Interface:

1. Use Scenario Development – the outline of the steps that the user may perform to accomplish some of the work.

2. Interface Structure Design – this defines the main components of the interface, as well as the way in which these components can provide functionality.

3. Interface Standards Design – the basic elements that can be found across many reports, screens, and forms within the system.

4. Interface Design Prototyping – this can be either a simulation or a mock-up of a screen, report, or form.

5. Interface Evaluation – the purpose of an evaluation is to figure out the best way to improve the interface design.

User Experience (UX)

It seems that people tend to use UI and UX interchangeably, but even though they are closely related, they represent two very different things.

User experience is, in fact, part of the UI design that is focused on the level of user computer experience. Think about it. A system can be used by both experts and novices. Novice users will most likely appreciate having the *ease of learning*, while experts will want to have the *ease of use*.

In many cases, these two complement each other and can lead to the same design, however, sometimes there are trade-offs. For instance, new users may want the ability to see all menu functions, while experts appreciate having fewer, well organized menus.

That is why it's important to pay a great deal of attention to the conceptual aspect of the UX when creating the UI design – so you can ensure customer satisfaction.

Database (DB) Design

Database design is one of the fundamental things in the process of system design and system development. If the database design is done correctly, then the system design and later, the system implementation will give little or no trouble at all. But what is *correct*? Here are some tips for executing an effective data design to help you create a killer database design:

The Nature of Your System

When beginning to create the database design, the first thing that you need to analyze, is the nature of your system. Many developers make the huge mistake of not thinking about the nature of the system they are designing and then face many issues later. Let's say that you want to design the database for your new application. The first thing you need to think about is "Is the application transactional or analytical"?

This is very important because if your application is transactional, your users will be more interested in CRUD (Creating, Reading, Updating, Deleting records). The name for this type of database is OLTP.
If the application is analytical, then the users will be more interested in analysis, reporting, forecasting. The name for this type of database is OLAP.

Break It Down

Make your life easier and break the data into <u>logical</u> pieces. Notice how I've emphasized 'logical'. It's because people usually overdo this step and try to deconstruct everything. Make sure to think things through.

Beware of Duplicate and Non-Uniform Data

Duplicate data can be tedious, but if it is non-uniform, then it can cause massive confusion. Imagine you have "2nd standard" and "second standard". This is the result of poor data entry or validation and any reports generated from this data will show each as a separate entity.

Watch Out for the Separators

If you have data with separators, you will need to be careful and avoid the "repeating groups", such as milk/chocolate, milk/banana, and chocolate/banana. You can create a separate table and create the many-to-many relationships there.

Be Sure to Maintain Your Data

Once you design your data, it needs to be operationally maintained. You need to observe the performance of the system closely and make sure to reorganize when it falls under the acceptable level. This is the single most important thing when it comes to your data.

Chapter 3:

Scalable Architecture and Distributed Systems

Scalable system design is something that you cannot escape on your system design interview. No matter what the interviewer might ask you, chances are, it will be related to the same concept – scalable system design. But before we start peeling the many layers of scalable system design and try to understand its complex architecture, let us first explain what *scalable* actually means.

The Scalability Behind Systems

If your system is *scalable* that means that it is capable to handle a growing amount of work. Since technology advances rapidly, you can understand why experience in scalable systems is something you should be familiar with when interviewing for a tech job.

Returning to the definition, a system is scalable when it is still able to increase its output, even after its load has increased and resources have been added.

Since everybody seems to have at least one computer these days, you can understand the need for such systems – both the performance expectations, as well as the transaction volumes have grown impressively in the past two decades.

When it comes to large distributed systems, their size is only one aspect that should be considered. Perhaps even more important is the required effort for the system to maintain its efficiency under increased capacity. That is the scalability; however, scalability can really refer to different system parameters:

- How much traffic can the system handle?
- How easily can more storage capacity be added?
- How many transactions can be processed?

The Basics of System Design Architecture

Systems are complex. When thinking about their architecture, there are a lot of things to consider:

- What are the system's pieces?
- How do these pieces fit together?
- What are the optimal trade-offs?

While investing in scaling before it is needed is not the best business strategy, having a solid understanding of the system design is truly beneficial as it can save a lot of time and energy for system developers.

All large applications and websites are focused on the same core factors: services, redundancy, and partitions.

Services

When we design scalable systems, it is important to think of the large system as a unit of smaller systems. Thinking about each part of the system as its own service will help separate the functionality and develop a better design. The systems that are designed this way are known to have Service-Oriented Architecture (SOA).

Let's imagine for a second a system where people can upload images to one central server, from where the images can be requested via link (ie: Flickr). However, let's keep it simple and imagine that the system can only do two things:

1. It can upload your images to the central server
2. It can query for your images

Now, let's see where we can find the services here. In the example above, all of the images are processed by the central server, however, as the need for scaling increases, so will the need to break the two main abilities of the system into services.

Deconstructing a system into services can help us prevent further issues. For instance, once our image system becomes heavily used, it will be much easier to have it deconstructed and solve problems independently.

Redundancy

In order to survive failure, an application or a website must have redundancy of the data and services. Imagine that there is one copy of a file and that copy gets lost. That would mean losing that file permanently. If you have redundant copies, on the other hand, losing the file would not be as devastating.

Redundancy in a system is a very important factor. It provides a backup which is a lifesaver in a crisis and dramatically reduces the chance of failure.

An important part is the *shared-nothing architecture*. Within this architecture, there is no 'central brain', as each node can operate independently. This increases the system's stability and makes it much more resistant to failure.

Partitions

Large sets of data cannot usually fit on a single server. In that case, partitions are needed.
If an operation requires many different sources and performance is suffering, additional capacity is required.

In either of these two situations you can do one of two choices: scale vertically or scale horizontally.

To scale vertically means to enrich a single server with additional resources. For instance, for large data sets, this can mean adding an additional hard drive. In the other example, this can mean moving the operation to a larger server.

To scale horizontally means to add more nodes. In the case of large data sets, this can mean to transfer some of the data to another server. In the other example, this can mean to load the operation across different nodes. The best way to scale horizontally is to break your services into *partitions*. Partitioning is a great technique that can bring added capacity.

The Building Blocks

Now that we have covered the core concepts and principles, let's dive into something more challenging – scaling access to the data.\

Fortunately, there are a couple of options that, when employed, can make your life a lot easier. We are about to discover the most common ways in which you can make your data a lot faster.

Caching

Caches are based on the idea that *"the recently requested data will be requested again"*. They are like short-term memories that - even having limited space - are usually faster than the original source of data. They exist in all architecture levels, however, caches are usually found at those levels that are nearest to the end, where they're used to do a quick data return.

But how can caches make the data faster? If we place a cache directly on the request layer node, that enables the storage of the response data, meaning that, when services are made, the cached nodes will return the local call quickly. If we expand the request layer to a couple of nodes, it is very likely that each of the nodes will have their own caches.

Consistent Hashing

When it comes to improving the scalability and increasing the storage architecture of a system, this is called *consistent hashing*. Consistent hashing is super important for distributed systems because:

1. It provides elastic scaling (dynamic addition of servers) for cache servers
2. It scales out storage node sets such as NoSQL database

But why do we need consistent hashing? Let's say that you want to make a scalable data backend with some database for your web application – let's call it 'x'. So, your goal is to design the database storage system in a way that will allow you to:

- Distribute the incoming queries among database 'x'
- Add or remove data servers dynamically
- Move the minimum data between the servers when you add or remove data servers

That means that you need to send each query to a particular server. The best approach is to:

1. Take a look at the incoming data in order to generate the hash key: `hashValue = HashFunction(Key)`.
2. Find out which server you need to send the data to by taking the HashValue's (%) modulo with the number of current servers in database 'x': `serverIndex = hashValue % x`.

There are, however, some drawbacks to this method that will need to be addressed later such as, horizontally scaling and non-uniform data distribution. Once that is addressed, your system will improve dramatically.

Consistent hashing is a topic that your interviewer may ask you about during your SDI. And while the theory is rather easy to explain, when it comes to using consistent hashing, here is what you need to know:

During your SDI, use consistent hashing only if:

- You have a data cluster and need to scale them up (or down) depending on the traffic load (ie: adding more servers during Christmas when there is extra traffic).
- You have a multiple cache servers that need to be scaled up or down elastically, depending on the traffic.

The CAP Theorem

Thanks to the progress of technology, ever-growing performance requests on applications, and massive global computing, horizontal scaling has become a real necessity in recent years.

Unfortunately, relieving the systems of the massive load is not the only thing scaling horizontally can do. These benefits come at a cost. That cost is called complexity.

Today, the distributed systems bring more factors into performance than they did before. Data records are known to vary across nodes, single failure points can destroy the up-time of the systems, and network issues tend to swoop in when least expected.

In the late 90s, Eric Brewer came up with the CAP theorem, as an attempt to explore a much wider space of design than the traditional systems at that time. His theorem remains as one of the best techniques for improving distributed systems.

The CAP Theorem is as follows:

Any distributed and network system can only have <u>two of three</u> preferred properties:

- *Consistency (C) – means having an updated data copy*
- *High Availability (A) – means having highly available data*
- *Tolerance of the **P**artitions in the network (P)*

To put it simply, the CAP theorem says that you cannot have consistency, availability, and partition tolerance simultaneously, but that trade-offs should be made for the desired performance to be achieved and the task to be executed successfully. For instance, if availability and consistency are super important, in that case you cannot partition the data. Or if you must partition the data and have consistency, then availability will be suffer.

However, if you think about it, it is availability (A) vs. consistency (C). Why? Because every system always needs availability and consistency. Since partitioning is a much rarer occurrence, systems usually have A and C all the time. So really, that's not an option. However, when partitioning must be done, this means either A or C suffers. When put this way, it seems like it is A vs C.

Chapter 4:

Taking Care of Bottlenecks

B*ottlenecks,* roadblocks, obstacles, or problems – whatever term we use to describe the issues we face along the way, they are not a good thing.

A bottleneck is just that – a problem that we face during a process when the input comes a lot faster than the following step can use it to create the output.

Pretty much any system has at least minor bottlenecks. If every server is running at full capacity, the system will most likely start accumulating processes. And while the server that stalls the longest is most likely to have a bottleneck, that is not always the case.

There are a lot of reasons why bottlenecks may occur. For instance, it could be that several clients share the same device, or that maybe the device is connected to one port, but demands higher capacity. Most system design issues occur as a result of the length of time needed to design, program and test, as well as from the limited resources that are used to satisfy the demand.

Identifying the bottlenecks and finding out where the 'choke point' is, is an essential thing if you want to improve the efficiency of your system. Unfortunately, as simple as it sounds, bottlenecks are not that easy to detect.

It is normal for your system design to have a bottleneck or two, given the constraint. And that is just fine because no one can get the system up and running at once.

If your design is a high-level one, think about what bottlenecks it might have. Perhaps it just needs a load balancer so it can handle the requests more efficiently. Or maybe, your data set is large and needs to be distributed on different machines.

The most important thing is to make sure that it is scalable, so that you can improve and resolve whatever problem with some of the most popular tools and techniques.

But remember, resolving bottlenecks is almost always a trade-off. You will fix one at the expense of another.

During your system design interview, you might also be asked about bottlenecks, and that might be a trick question. Just remember what is important:

- The system must be scalable
- It will most likely need a load balancer
- The data will most likely need to be distributed
- If the data is slow it will need memory caching
- Bottlenecks are usually trade-offs. They might negatively impact some other part of the system. It is important to measure the impact and decide whether the problem is worth solving. Make sure to mention that during the interview.

Chapter 5:

Effective Design

Now that we have covered most concepts, the next question is, how do I know if my design is effective or not? Well, here is the thing. There aren't exactly good or bad designs – only those that work and others that don't work. The answer here is clear. If your design is working without tons of bottlenecks, then yes, you have a proper design. If not, go back and try to figure out what you did wrong and what you might improve.

However, you need to know the 'formula' for creating an effective design. As a recap of everything we've covered, follow the tips below for an effective system design and be sure to touch on these points during your interview.

- Understand the workload conditions of the system that you are designing. This can be dimensions of growth (data volume, number of users, volume of transactions, etc.) Also, understand the target measurements (throughput, response time, etc.)

- Understand who your customers are. You need to know exactly who your priority is. The importance of traffic should be ranked so you can know who you can allow yourself to sacrifice in case you will not be able to handle them all.

- Scale horizontally, not vertically. Always strive to seek the solution by horizontal scaling first.

That way you will be able to add a cheaper machine, and not upgrade vertically, to a more powerful one.

- Make sure your codes are simple and modular. Code modularity is a number one priority. It shouldn't be sacrificed for any reason, even if the performance of the system depends on it. That will give you the chance to swap out code and experiment much more efficiently, which, in turn, will lead to quick optimization.

- Measure your bottlenecks. If you cannot pinpoint the problem, write performance test units while you collect 'fine grain' performance data. You may also set up a performance lab if you want to. That will help you make end-to-end measurements of the performance.

- Always plan for growth. Capacity planning must be done on a regular basis. Make it a habit to collect statistics of usage and predict the rate of growth.

Chapter 6:

Things You Need to Know Prior to the Interview

Preparing for a system design interview is not only intimidating, but scary too. There is no particular pattern, certain rules, nor a specific template that you should prepare for. There is only the interviewer, yourself, and your knowledge. But that is not the hardest part. The interview is open-ended, meaning that there isn't a right or wrong answer. This can make the preparation process even more overwhelming.

However, just because your technical knowledge is about to be on display doesn't mean that you should feel vulnerable. Let this chapter help you prepare for the long-awaited SDI without a shred of stress.

What is Evaluated During SDI?

You have probably run through the interview a hundred times in your head. How you will sit, what you are going to say, the tone of your voice, etc. But I bet in those those hundred replays, that you did not play the role of the interviewer. Let's consider what the interviewer expects from the candidates.

During the interview, you are asked to solve some open-ended problems. That means that you are the one that should lead the conversation. Discussion is the single most important element of this interview. Try to minimize any awkward silence between your answers. The interviewer expects you to take the lead and maintain the direction of the conversation.

Remember, it is not only your knowledge that is evaluated, but also your communication skills and ability to solve problems.

Go Back to the Basics

Although you may prepare for complex questions, know that you also may be asked some pretty simple questions. It wouldn't hurt to go through the simple and basic concepts to refresh your memory:

- Abstraction
- Database
- Network
- Concurrency
- Operating System
- Machine Learning

Remember, it is important to understand the basic concept behind more complicated ideas. You should never answer with "I don't know". For instance, even if you don't know *how* to implement neural networks, you should still be able to explain what they are or when they are appropriate to use.

Take the Top-Down Approach

Avoid getting into details too early, as you may lose your audience and create confusion. Instead of shooting for the solution immediately, spend some time working out the problem first. This is what is expected from you. Most system-design questions will be too general for you to solve immediately, and you are required to start with some high-level ideas and then figure out the details gradually.

Do a Mock Interview

Since it can be difficult to prepare for an interview by yourself, I suggest you seek professional help. If you know any experts who can practice the interview with you, that would be a huge advantage.

This way, you will get to spend time communicating and discussing ideas, which is great practice.

If you don't have anyone to practice with, don't worry. There are sites out there which allow you to have mock interviews with experts from Google, Amazon, Facebook, Microsoft, Linkedin, and other top-tier firms.

Chapter 7:

Steps to Approach Your SDI

Although you may think you will need luck to pass the interview, you will only need thorough preparation and proper knowledge combined with excellent communication skills to articulate your thoughts.

When companies ask about designing systems, they are usually referring to large, distributed ones. With your attained knowledge (both practical and theoretical) and what we have covered so far, the only thing you need to remember are the steps to approaching the interview:

Step 1: Gather Requirements

One of the biggest mistakes that interviewees make, is that they are so focused on scaling the system that they forget to think about the actual system. You cannot scale anything if you do not have a system, so the first thing you need to be concerned with is finding the scope of the problem.

Clarifying any uncertainties from the start is critical. So, if you are asked to design YouTube, for instance, your first questions should be something like this:

- Who can view videos?
- Who can upload videos?
- Who can comment on the videos?
- Can you subscribe to uploaders?
- Can the users search for videos?
- How many total views are there?

- How many daily views are there?

The questions above are just examples. Remember, you are trying to understand the scope; you don't need to worry about handling the videos.

Step 2: Defining the System Interface

If your requirements have been gathered and the API (Application Programming Interface) is exposed by the system, you are almost half done. Make sure to define what are the APIs that are expected from the system.

Step 3: Back-of-the-Envelope Capacity Estimation

Having an idea of how large your system is going to be, is the perfect place to start. When focusing on scaling or caching later, this will be a huge help.

- What is the scale that is expected from the system?
- How much storage should you have?
- What it the expected network bandwidth usage?

Step 4: Define the Data Model

If you manage to define the data model in the early stages, that will clarify how the data will flow into the system's components. Besides, it will be an important guide later when you will think about partitioning.

- Which database should the system use?
- NoSQL or MySQL?
- What should the blob storage be like?

Step 5: The High-Level Design

Draw a simple block diagram that represents the main components of your system. You can use the System Design Primer as a guide. Make sure that your diagram has all of the needed components to actually solve the problem from end to end.

Step 6: Dig into the Details

Dig deeper by two or three components. Again, you can use the primer from earlier, however, keep in mind that it is the feedback of the interviewer that should guide you towards the parts that he or she wants you to collaborate. Be prepared to give different approaches, their pros and cons, and a justification for your selected approach.

Don't forget – there is no right answer. The only thing that you need consider are the trade-offs and constraints of each option.

- Should the data be stored on one database?
- How should we distribute the multiple databases?
- At which layer should a cache be introduced?
- Which of the components need load balancing?

Step 7: Beware the Bottlenecks

Try to discuss bottlenecks and find the right approach to resolve them.

- Is there a single point of failure?
- Do we have backups of our data?

- Do we have copies of the servers that are running?
- How is the service performance monitored?
- Are we alerted when important components fail?

Chapter 8:

The Most Common Questions

Designing Large Scale Distributed Systems is a standard procedure that will measure your software engineering skills. It is only natural that you would want to know what you will be asked to design. You don't need a crystal ball to peek into the future. With these most common interview questions, you will equip yourself with the confidence to give the right answer to any kind of question.

Design TinyURL or bitly (URL shortening service)

You will be given a pretty long URL and will be asked to design a specific service that will generate a much shorter version of it.

If you are asked that during your SDI, here is what you should discuss:

How to generate the unique ID for each one of the URLs?
- How to generate the IDs at scale?
- How can you support the custom short URLs?
- How to redirect the service handle?
- How the track the stats of the clicks?
- How can you delete those URLs that have expired?

Design Netflix, YouTube, or Twitch

You will be asked to design a service that will be storing, as well as transmitting, millions of videos.

If you are asked that during your SDI, here is what you should discuss:

- How to efficiently store and transmit data?
- How would users add comments?
- How would the statistics about the videos (such as views, votes, etc.) be recorded?

Design WhatsApp or Facebook Messenger

If you are asked how to design a messenger, be sure to discuss:

- How would the one-on-one conversations be designed?
- When should you send push notifications?
- What would happen if the user is not online?

Design Dropbox or Google Drive

Make sure to discuss:

- How would the users upload and view the files?
- How would they share them?
- How would the permission for sharing be tracked?
- How would multiple users be allowed to edit a single document?

Design Facebook, Instagram, or Twitter

When you are designing a social media platform that has millions of users, you need to discuss the following:

- How would the newsfeed be generated?
- How would users be able to post and search for posts?
- How can users search other users?
- How would the social graph be generated?

Design Uber

When you are designing a ride-share service, you should discuss:

- How would you store all the geographical locations of the drivers?
- How would the location updates be handled?
- How to match the customers with the nearest ride?

Design Type Ahead (a search engine service)

When designing type ahead you would have a service that can suggest the top 10 searched items. Besides that, be sure to discuss:

- How would you keep the data up-to-date?
- How would you store the previous queries?
- How to match the string that is already typed?

Design Web Crawler

Here, you would need to design a service that is scalable and that can crawl the web, to gather hundreds of millions of documents.

- How would new pages be found?
- How would you prioritize the pages that change dynamically?
- How to make sure that the crawler doesn't get stuck on the same domain?

Conclusion

I hope that this book gave you a better understanding of an SDI, a clear idea of what to expect, and tips on how to prepare accordingly.

Now that you know how to nail your System Design Interview, the next step is to use the knowledge and skills gained from this book to get the position you deserve.

Did you find this book helpful? Leave a review and let others know. Your feedback is greatly appreciated.

Thank you and happy interviewing!